Research It!

Slavery and the Slave Trade

Richard Spilsbury

Heinemann Library
Chicago, Illinois

www.heinemannraintree.com
Visit our website to find out more information about Heinemann-Raintree books.

To order:
☎ Phone 888-454-2279
🖳 Visit www.heinemannraintree.com to browse our catalog and order online.

Edited by Susan Crean and Rebecca Vickers
Designed by Steven Mead
Illustrated by Jeff Edwards
Picture research by Ruth Blair
Production by Victoria Fitzgerald
Originated by Capstone Global Library Ltd
Printed and bound in China by South China Printing Company Ltd

14 13 12 11 10
10 9 8 7 6 5 4 3 2 1

Library of Congress Cataloging-in-Publication Data
Spilsbury, Richard, 1963-
  Slavery and the slave trade / Richard Spilsbury.
    p. cm. -- (Research it!)
  Includes bibliographical references and index.
  ISBN 978-1-4329-3495-8 (hc)
  1. Slave trade--History. 2. Slavery--History. I. Title.
  HT975.S65 2009
  306.3'6209--dc22

2009008757

Acknowledgments
The author and publishers are grateful to the following for permission to reproduce copyright material: Alamy: p. **39** (© INTERFOTO Pressebildagentur); Bridgeman Art Library: p. **9** (Private Collection/The Stapleton Collection); © Corbis: p. **47** (Bettmann); Getty Images, pp. **27 bottom**, **29** (Bridgeman Art Library/American School), **27 top** (Bridgeman Art Library/English School), **12**, **48** (Hulton Archive), **6** (Hulton Archive/Stringer), **35** (Time Life Pictures/Stringer); Mary Evans Picture Library: pp. **31** (DEAGOSTINI EDITORE), **13**; Rex Features: pp. **5** (Fotex), **37** (Roger-Viollet); © Shutterstock and © iStockphoto: design features.

The main cover image of a group of African Americans aboard the USS *Vermont* is reproduced with permission of © Corbis. The background images are reproduced with permission of the following: © iStockphoto (© Sharon Day, © Royce DeGrie, © Olena Druzhynina, © Boros Emese, © Darek Niedzieski) and © shutterstock (© Sascha Burkard, © Lars Lindblad, © javaman, © Irina Tischenko).

We would like to thank Stewart Ross for his invaluable help in the preparation of this book.

Every effort has been made to contact copyright holders of material reproduced in this book. Any omissions will be rectified in subsequent printings if notice is given to the publisher.

Contents

Some words are printed in bold, **like this**. You can find out what they mean by looking in the glossary.

Researching the Past

Slavery and the slave trade in the 18th and 19th centuries is a major topic in history studies. It is an episode from the past, yet there are many reasons why the topic remains important today. Many people study slavery because they feel strongly about the rights and wrongs of the topic. It is a good example of how people who promote **human rights** can create change: in this case, the change led to the end of the slave trade.

There are also strong links between life today and the times when slavery occurred. For example, the wealth of the United States is partly a result of the trade in goods produced using slave labor on **colonial plantations**. For some people, the links are even more relevant. The African-American and Afro-Caribbean descendants of slaves are today an integral part of the rich cultural mix of peoples in countries such as the United States.

There is an enormous wealth of fascinating information on the topic of slavery and the slave trade in books, on the Internet, and from many other sources. This book does not aim to fill in all the gaps in your knowledge. Its aim instead is to introduce the techniques and approaches you will need to find out more and answer questions about slavery and the slave trade in Africa, North America, and the Caribbean.

Why research?

People may research a topic because they are inquisitive. They want to know and understand the world around them now and in the past. But sometimes research is undertaken to find specific information to help with an essay, exam, or oral presentation. But there is more to research than just finding out answers. The process of research draws on many skills and techniques. Once you have found evidence, you need to sort, evaluate, and understand it to help answer your questions and fill out your knowledge.

Broad and narrow research

Research can be time-consuming or relatively easy. Sometimes you can spend a long time finding a small amount of useful information, but at other times it may happen much more quickly. A key part of the research process is first figuring out what you need to know about a topic. If it is a broad subject area, such as the history of slavery, it helps to narrow the focus of your research.

Your first point of access into the wealth of information on slavery and the slave trade may be a library computer, where you can search the Internet or find out about the books on the shelves.

Slavery questions

Your research task may be to answer a particular question on slavery and the slave trade, or to research more general information. Here are a few examples:

- Imagine you could meet the owner of a transatlantic slave ship. What are some of the reasons the owner might give to defend the slave trade?
- Was the U.S. **Civil War** fought to free slaves?
- Compare the lives of and opportunities for free blacks in the northern United States with those of southern free blacks.
- Why did the United States allow slavery after it made the slave trade illegal?
- How was the slave trade eventually **abolished**?

If you research too broad a subject area, you may find so much information that it becomes confusing. You may want to research specific information about people who helped abolish slavery, day-to-day conditions for slaves, or public reports from the time about slavery.

Researching specific topics will help you to understand the bigger picture. But you may also be asked to research a specific, narrow question, such as, "When was slavery abolished in the West Indies?" In that case, it may help to broaden your research to understand the context of that event. For example, you might research key events in the history of slavery in the United Kingdom (the West Indies were a British colony) to see where **abolition** fits into the story.

Primary and secondary sources

Books and other resources in libraries and on the Internet are often the most useful sources for your research. Generally sources are divided into two categories—primary and secondary.

It is both fascinating and shocking to discover more about a time when many people considered it acceptable to capture, chain, and force others to work for them as slaves.

Primary sources are original, firsthand accounts of events. They provide evidence of something happening, being said, or thought. Primary sources include diaries and newspaper reports written by people at the time of an event or not long after it happened.

Secondary sources are created after an event. They use different primary sources to explain an event. They include history textbooks and biographies of famous people. Secondary sources often mention or quote primary sources. Secondary sources are usually books, which are generally easy to access compared to one-of-a-kind primary sources, such as letters or diaries. You should use a mix of primary and secondary sources in historical research whenever possible.

Slavery sources

Types	Primary	Secondary
	Letters, diaries, autobiographies, photos, art, documentary films, legal documents, and newspapers	History textbooks, historical movies, biographies, photos, and art
When was it made?	At the time of an event, or soon after	Created after an event, sometimes a long time after it happened
Who created it?	Someone who saw or heard an event himself or herself; it may express an opinion or argument about an event	Someone who wasn't there, often using a range of primary or other secondary sources; it may express an opinion or argument about a past event
Rarity	Often one-of-a-kind, or rare	More commonly available

What Is Slavery and the Slave Trade?

It is useful to start off your research into slavery and the slave trade by getting an overview of the topic. An overview provides you with a basic understanding of the topic from which to extend your research. This will help you decide what else you need to look for online or in print. You will need to read or look in several secondary sources, including history books and encyclopedias, to build up your own understanding. This section of this book provides a simple overview of the topic that may help in your research.

Through research, you will find that most sources agree about what slavery is. Slavery is the practice of owning people to do work. Slaves do not have basic freedoms, such as being able to act or speak without restraint, and are not paid for their work. Often slave owners treat slaves cruelly in order to force them to work or obey commands. Slavery is now associated with the 17th to 19th centuries, but in fact the practice is thousands of years old.

Slavery in ancient times

Slaves were common in the great ancient civilizations of Egypt, Greece, and Rome. For example, many slaves in ancient Egypt were involved in agriculture, carried out heavy work, such as building pyramids, or served in the homes of rich people. Many were captured during wars in regions bordering the Nile River, such as Sudan and Ethiopia.

In Rome, which was the capital of the Roman Empire about 2,000 years ago, around one-third of the population was made up of slaves. Some of these slaves were gladiators trained to fight for entertainment. Not all slaves carried out backbreaking or dangerous physical work. Some were scribes (expert writers), physicians, or accountants.

The start of the slave trade

People sold or traded slaves to others to make money. For example, there were slave markets in ancient Rome. However, the large-scale slave trade involving the capture and transportation of slaves began in the **Middle Ages**.

The Islamic empires spread from the Middle East through Africa between the 8th and 15th centuries, in part to get useful, valuable resources. African slaves were considered a trading resource. Slave raiders established slave

The first commercial contacts between Europeans and Africans began in the 15th century. In the late 19th century, some Europeans used the campaign against the slave trade as an excuse to colonize Africa.

routes—paths and roads they used to take their numerous captives to ports for transportation to North Africa and Europe. But not all slave raiders were from outside Africa. In West Africa, rival ethnic groups sometimes took slaves as prisoners of war, payment for a debt, or punishment for a crime.

Slaves as servants

In the early days of the slave trade—for example, in Portugal and its colonies in the 15th century—many slaves were **indentured servants**. This means that slaves were freed after a fixed period of service. While in service or after they had finished, slaves were sometimes **baptized**, became educated, and lived among and married into working classes of society. A slave's children were born free even if their parents had limited freedom.

Portuguese slavery

Some of the earliest European explorers in Africa were Portuguese. They set up colonies on islands off the coast of Africa. They farmed sugarcane on the islands, which grew well in the warm climate. The Portuguese started to trade goods with West African leaders in return for slaves to work the fields. By the end of the 16th century, the Portuguese had enslaved 25,000 Africans to work on sugar plantations.

Slavery in the New World

Around the end of the 17th century, the nature of slavery started to change. British colonies, such as Virginia in the **New World**, made laws saying that slaves and their children were the property of owners and could be traded. This is called **chattel slavery**. The advantage to slave owners was that they could legally get free work from a slave's whole family or money from the sale of several slaves, rather than one.

The slave trade had expanded following the arrival of Europeans in the New World. Slavery first emerged in the New World along the northeast coast of South America and in the West Indies. The Spanish and Portuguese set up colonies in these regions, where gold and silver mines and sugar plantations flourished. The colonizers enslaved **indigenous** peoples to work in these industries, but the supply of workers soon dried up. This is because many local people died from diseases they caught from the Europeans. New World colonies began to import African slaves to do the work instead. Soon other countries, including Great Britain, France, and Sweden, started to establish colonies in the New World. They, too, brought in African slaves to work.

Sugar was the main New World crop at first, but later silk, coffee, and tobacco became important. These farming industries grew as demand for these products increased in Europe. For example, people in London developed a taste for sugar in drinks.

Slave data

Some captains and surgeons on slave ships kept careful records of the slaves they transported across the Atlantic. Their logbooks reveal how many slaves got sick from diseases and died on the long voyages. These records are useful to historians interested in counting the human cost of the triangular trade (see page 11). But there is still great uncertainty about exactly how many people were enslaved and transported. Estimates of the number of Africans transported vary from 11 to 20 million. At least 1.5 million died on the journey. Slave transportation records are a valuable primary source to use in researching the slave trade.

The triangular trade

The regular pattern of trade between Europe, the Americas, and Africa was called the **triangular trade**. Sailing ships would travel southwest from Europe to Africa, helped by the strong winds and currents in that direction. They were loaded with goods such as copper, cloth, and guns. Once the goods were unloaded for trading, enslaved Africans were loaded in the holds. When a ship was full, it would set sail to the Americas, helped by strong northwesterly winds. This leg of the triangle was called the **Middle Passage** and took up to eight weeks.

The crowded conditions for slaves on these slave ships were appalling. Infectious diseases such as dysentery, which causes severe diarrhea and sickness, spread fast, and many slaves died on the journey. In the Americas, the slave cargo was unloaded and then goods for sale in Europe were loaded for the journey back across the Atlantic.

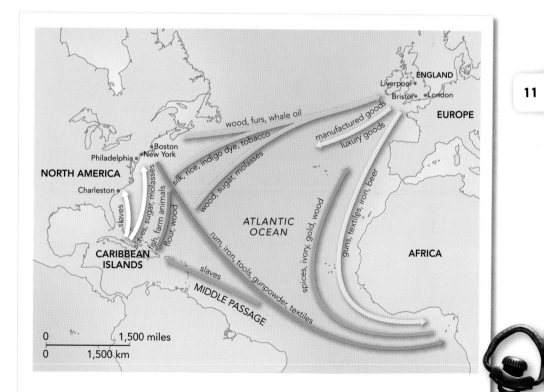

This map summarizes the flow of goods and slaves in the transatlantic triangular trade.

From slave ship to plantations

Slaves who survived the Middle Passage had hard times to endure in the New World. Typically they were sold at slave auctions to plantation owners. The owners tended to choose the slaves who looked healthiest and strongest. Once on plantations slaves were "seasoned," or made ready for work. At best this was training for work on the plantation by experienced slaves—for example, being taught how to work in "gangs." At worst it was cruel treatment to make the slaves obey any order and live in fear of their owners. Slaves were routinely injured, whipped, chained, and denied food or water. Some historians estimate that 30 percent of imported Africans died of diseases or cruel treatment during "seasoning."

Slave owners used chains and metal collars to prevent slaves from trying to escape. There are many online archives of slave photographs to use in your research, such as http://afroamhistory.about.com/od/slavery/ig/Slavery-Photographs-and-Images/.

Work on plantations varied according to the crops grown. For sugarcane, the strongest gangs cut the tough canes, while other gangs stacked and loaded, crushed, boiled, and refined (purified) the sugar ready for sale. Other slaves had domestic jobs, such as cooks, housemaids, or stable workers for the owner and his family. Slaves usually worked from dawn until dusk—and even longer during busy harvest times.

Slaves in the United States

After the Revolutionary War ended in 1783, the 13 former British colonies along the Atlantic coast became the independent United States. Settlers started to move west and south across the continent. Some of the first settlers were black, including freed slaves who had fought against the British. The settlers formed new towns and farms. Slavery in the South was mainly based in agriculture, due to the warm climate in which important cash crops, including cotton, could grow. In the cooler northern states there was less intensive agriculture, so slaves tended to work as domestic help.

The economics of slavery

Slavery was an essential part of the U.S., UK, French, and other economies. The slave trade brought great wealth to individuals and cities, such as New York City, the British ports of Liverpool and Bristol, and the French port of Nantes. The slavery industry created new trade links and played a part in the **Industrial Revolution**. The slave trade provided work for hundreds of thousands of sailors, traders, and others. By the end of the 18th century, however, more people began to question the economics, as well as the morality, of the slave trade. Shipping and buying slaves was becoming expensive, and some runaway slaves were causing revolts.

A family of house slaves is shown cheerfully serving their rich owner's guests in a 19th-century domestic scene from the southern United States. In your research, you can see if the evidence supports the truth of images like this one.

New technology

In the southern United States, cotton became a major crop from the end of the 18th century after the invention of the cotton gin. This technology was 50 times faster at separating the useful cotton fibers, which were made into cloth, from the sticky cotton seeds. Cotton became profitable to grow in large quantities. Plantations spread throughout the South, and plantation owners purchased more African slaves to tend the crops.

The end of the slave trade

At the end of the 18th century, people started to speak out against the transatlantic slave trade as being **inhumane** and illegal, including those in religious groups, such as the Quakers. People read newspaper reports of Quaker speeches and accounts of the conditions on slave ships and life on plantations. Many ex-slaves, who had been freed after fighting on the British side during the Revolutionary War, were living in Britain. British politicians, such as William Wilberforce, started to campaign for the abolition, or banning by law, of the slave trade.

In your research you might want to read the speeches of Wilberforce and other early abolitionists. After the United Kingdom's abolition of the slave trade in 1807, British ships were no longer allowed to transport African slaves. Nevertheless, slaves in Britain were not granted freedom until 1833.

North and South

In the United States, the transatlantic slave trade supposedly ended in 1808. However, slavery itself continued in the South. The cotton trade boomed in the early 19th century as world demand for cotton increased, and slavery was an important part of the plantation-based economy. With no new slaves from Africa arriving in the country, an internal U.S. slave trade developed. When slaves had children, they became slaves, too. U.S. slave traders grew rich by purchasing slaves from port cities and selling them to plantations in the Deep South. Slave families were routinely split up in the process.

There was growing disagreement between northern and southern states about slavery. Those in the North had newly industrialized cities and societies with a wide range of immigrant workers, and they banned slavery. Many slaves in the North were **emancipated**, or legally free, so these were called the **free states**. The differences between free states and **slave states** was one reason for the U.S. Civil War (1861–65). The U.S. government banned all slavery in 1863, and the northern Union states won the war in 1865.

Life after slavery

Life for freed slaves, especially in the South, was far from easy after they were freed. Most were too poor to buy farmland, so they became sharecroppers. This meant they took on and worked portions of plantation land, and received seeds and equipment in return for half their crop. In many places black people were **segregated**, or separated, from white people. For example, they could not do the same jobs or go to the same schools. They had to use different parts of shared facilities, such as buses and restaurants.

Legal segregation persisted in the South until the mid-20th century. Campaigning for equal rights eventually gave African Americans greater equality and opportunities. One major example of the change since the time of slavery is the election of Barack Obama as president in 2008.

Timeline of slavery and the slave trade

1502	First reported African slaves are taken to the New World.
1562	John Hawkins becomes the first British slave trader.
1619	The first Africans are taken to the British North American colonies.
1699	About 80 percent of the Caribbean population is enslaved Africans.
1789	One of the first slave autobiographies, by Olaudah Equiano, is published in London.
1791	The British Parliament rejects William Wilberforce's bill to abolish the slave trade.
1793	U.S. inventor Eli Whitney invents the cotton gin.
1794	The United States prohibits new slave boats from being equipped in U.S. ports.
1807	Slavery and the transatlantic slave trade are abolished in Britain.
1808	The United States bans the importation of new slaves.
1819	Britain stations a naval squadron on the West African coast to patrol against illegal slavers.
1820	U.S. law makes slave trading piracy, and therefore those found guilty face the death penalty; the U.S. Congress agrees to the Missouri Compromise, dividing states into pro- or anti-slavery.
1833	The British Parliament abolishes slavery in all its colonies.
1839	The *Amistad* slave boat rebellion occurs.
1849	Harriet Tubman escapes from the South to the North and establishes the **Underground Railroad**.
1858	William Yancey publicizes a Confederacy of southern states.
1860	Southern states start to **secede** (separate) from the northern Union states.
1861	The U.S. Civil War begins.
1863	The Emancipation Proclamation is issued by President Abraham Lincoln, declaring that all slaves in the parts of the United States rebelling against the Union are free.
1865	Slavery is banned in the United States under the 13th amendment to the Constitution.
1888	Slavery is banned in Brazil.

Getting Started

We all know the feeling. You have an assignment to complete or a big project to start. It seems like an enormous task. So, how do you begin?

What are you trying to research?

The most important thing to do at the start of research is to understand what you have to find out. Just like going on a vacation, in research you need to know your destination. Your research destinations are the varied questions you need to answer and topics you have to present. Some will require lots of information to address, while others will need less research. Read your assignment question or research topic carefully, and make sure you understand what will be required. For example, you might have to research the events building up to the abolition of slavery in the United States. This will obviously require both specific factual knowledge about the events and people involved and an overview of the context of slavery at that time.

You will have limits on how much time you can spend on your research, so focus your mind at the outset on what is needed. For example, don't waste time getting caught up in hours of research on a topic that will do little to help your final project. Stay focused on the task at hand.

What do you know already?

What do you know about slavery and the slave trade already? Before you begin any research, create a **mind map** of the topic. To make a mind map, start by writing down a central idea or keyword, such as "slavery" or "transatlantic slave trade." Then create lines from that idea to words or ideas around it that you associate with the topic, such as "slavery different from freedom," "the South," or "cotton plantation."

Sometimes you will know very detailed information, perhaps because you recently visited a slavery exhibition at a museum. You may be surprised by how much you know without ever having studied the topic. Your mind stores all kinds of pieces of information from books, movies, museum trips, and many other sources. Creating a mind map (see page 17) can help you recall them. Each bubble or branch of a mind map contains an idea. Try to link similar ideas as you remember them.

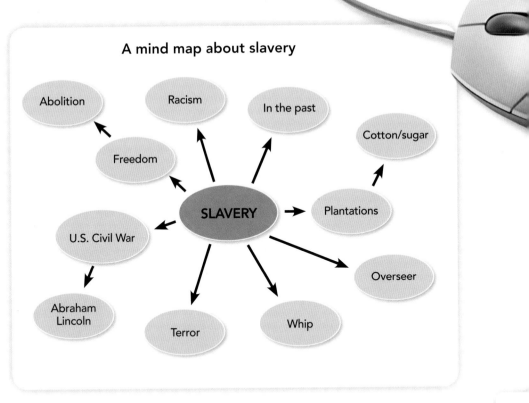

A mind map about slavery

- Abolition
- Racism
- In the past
- Cotton/sugar
- Freedom
- **SLAVERY**
- Plantations
- U.S. Civil War
- Overseer
- Abraham Lincoln
- Terror
- Whip

KWL chart

A **KWL chart** is a type of **graphic organizer** that can help you to focus your research at the beginning of the process. "KWL" stands for "Know/Want to know/Learn":

- What do you already **K**now at the start of your research?
- What do you **W**ant to know?
- What have you **L**earned during your research?

Topic: *Abolition of slavery in the United States*
Question: *Why was slavery abolished in the United States?*

What I **K**now	What I **W**ant to know	What I have **L**earned
Some people wanted to abolish slavery because it was cruel. *The slave trade was illegal.*	*How did owners treat their slaves? Who campaigned against slavery? What did Nat Turner do? Who was Frederick Douglass?*	(To be filled in when you answer your research questions)

Where to find information

Your next step is to look at secondary sources. The second chapter of this book provides one overview of slavery and the slave trade. It is a secondary source that condenses centuries of history into just a few pages. Other sources may have very different summaries of the same topic. Each source will be different in terms of what it considers important, how much detail it goes into, and other issues. You should look at several secondary sources to make sure you fully understand the events and background of your topic.

The best general secondary sources are usually reference books and online resources, such as research **databases** and websites. Reference books include encyclopedias with concise entries on a wide range of subjects. Well-known general subject encyclopedia sets in multiple volumes include *Encyclopedia Britannica* and *World Book*. There are single-volume encyclopedias and history encyclopedias that cover world history in general or focus more specifically on U.S. or British history. Since these two countries were so heavily involved with slavery and the slave trade, books on their history are likely to include information on the topic.

Other secondary sources include historical dictionaries and nonfiction books on particular topics.

Choosing your secondary sources

There are many reference books available in libraries and bookstores. A librarian or bookstore sales associate can direct you to where to find them. You might also use a library's computer records before checking the shelves. These will list the books that the library holds and allow you to search by author, by title, and by subject.

So, how do you know which books are best to use in your research? One thing to consider is the date of publication. Recent books will have the most up-to-date version of events. Since the slave trade ended in the 19th century, you might think that a book published since then will

Navigating a reference book

These are some of the ways to find your way around reference books:
- A to Z: Some books are arranged alphabetically by subject.
- Contents: A table of contents at the start of a book will let you browse the topics inside and then turn to the correct page.
- Index: Indexes at the end of a book are an alphabetical list of keywords. In some indexes, if you see italic page numbers, you will know where to look for illustrations on the subject.

contain all the events. However, attitudes toward the topic have changed greatly, and new research has been carried out. More modern books may present the topic in a more up-to-date way that is easier to understand.

Another aspect of reference books to consider is suitability. A young person's encyclopedia may not have enough detail to research the topic fully, and the language used may be too simple. On the other hand, encyclopedias for adults will probably be too complex and detailed.

Using the Internet

The Internet can be accessed at home, in school, or in a library by using a computer with an Internet connection. One way to use the Internet is by searching online research databases. Most schools have free access to some databases. Research databases are developed, and their information selected and checked for accuracy, with a specific audience in mind. As online research databases are often subscription services (where membership or payment is required), schools and public libraries join on behalf of their users. Ask your teacher or a librarian what is available for you to use, how to use it, and for a user name or password.

Search engines, such as Yahoo! and Google, will help you find websites on a subject. For example, if you type "slavery" into Google, it supplies more than 20 million results, though many will not be relevant to your needs.

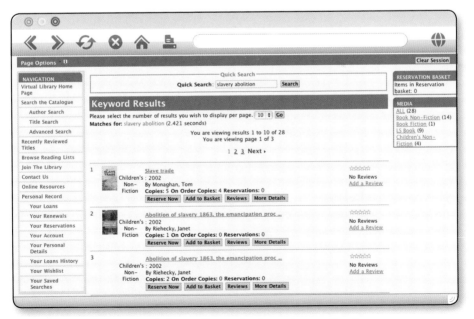

This example of a screengrab from a library database shows a list of titles found during a search for the keywords "slavery abolition."

This screengrab shows details from one title on a library database list.

In most libraries you can check who wrote a book, who published it, and when. On the Internet, it is not always obvious who wrote or published the information. Some online information on slavery has been carefully put together by expert historians and teachers, but some has been hurriedly done by non-experts with **biased** opinions on the topic. You can find mentions of "slavery" in online encyclopedias or on someone's personal weblog, or blog. A blog is like an online diary with people's thoughts on different subjects. In a blog with the topic of slavery, you might find information ranging from people who agree with racism to those who campaign against it.

How to search
It can be a problem when using search engine results to find those that are the most relevant and reliable. A way to do this is to use a subject directory. Subject directories provide links, organized in categories, to websites people have selected because they found them useful or of good quality. Subject directories are useful if you are not sure exactly what you are looking for. For example, visit www.dmoz.org and search for "slavery." The results include a short list of categories of websites, including "Society: History: By Region: Africa: Slavery." They also include a longer list of websites.

Another effective way to search is to use several words in a search engine. For example, perhaps you want to find out about 19th-century plantations in North Carolina. Most search engines will look for all of the words you include. Some allow you to put OR between the words to refine your search. Others let you put a phrase, such as "chattel slavery" or "North Carolina," in quotes so you only get sites that have those exact words in that order.

Web evaluation checklist

Here are some things to look for in websites that will help you to distinguish the good from the bad:

- Check the address: A website's address is also called its URL and contains clues about the website. For example, the characters at the end of a URL show the category of website. Government sites include .gov and educational sites end with .edu, while .com is a commercial site, or one that exists to make money, and may be biased in content.
- Check around the edges: If there are links on the website to "About us," "Our philosophy," "Background," or "About the authors," you can check who put the information together. Was it written by a respected academic or an unreliable fanatic?
- Question the quality: Are there **citations** to say where the website got its information? Does the website have good spelling and presentation? Are there links to other reliable sources of information?

Narrowing your web search results

If you do separate web searches for the three words <u>railroad</u>, <u>underground</u>, and <u>freedom</u>, you will get millions of results (see diagram below left). Hidden in this huge amount of information there are probably some relevant sources. However, when you input the words <u>underground railroad freedom</u> together, you get more focused resources (see diagram below right), many of them worth a look. You could narrow your search even further by adding another term, such as a geographic area like Virginia.

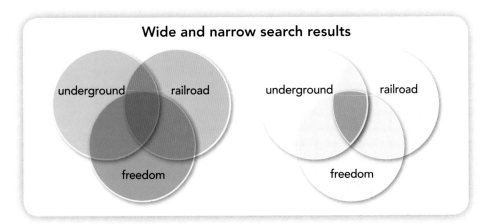

Wide and narrow search results

Finding information quickly

After you have found reference books and online sources that look like they might contain the sort of information you will need, how do you locate it? People whose jobs involve finding information in varying sources, such as librarians or teachers, do not have time to read everything. So, they use the techniques of **skimming** and **scanning** to find the specific information they need.

Skimming is when you find out what a source contains by reading or viewing only certain parts of the piece. Here is a skimming checklist:

- Read the title, the introduction or first paragraph, the first sentence of every other paragraph, and the summary or last paragraph. These will give you an overview of the information the piece contains.
- Focus on all headings or subheadings and any italic or bold words. This material is probably significant and may even be defined in a glossary or be linked to other parts of a website.
- Look at the pictures, charts, and graphs. Most publications select illustrations carefully, and it is likely any images will help your understanding of the subject.

Word definitions

Many sources have a glossary or, in the case of a web page, they might include underlined words that link to definitions. You will find different definitions depending on the age of reader for which the source is published and, of course, the author's interpretation of what a word means. Here are some different definitions for the word "slavery" from Internet sources:

"The institution or social practice of owning human beings as property, especially for use as forced laborers." http://en.wiktionary.org/wiki/slavery

"Keeping people as property, and requiring them to work under the domination of others." http://abolition.e2bn.org/glossary/view_glossary_0_S.html

"The practice of making a person work for no money and without the freedom to leave." www.mhschool.com/ss/ny/glossary/s.html

Scanning is slightly different from skimming. People use the technique of scanning to locate specific information including dates, names, and places. For example, you might want to answer the question, "What was William Lloyd Garrison's role in the abolition of slavery in the United States?" Therefore, you would scan entire sources to spot the words "abolition" or "Garrison" or "U.S. slavery." You would then read those parts of text more carefully to find more detailed information.

Taking notes

A pen and paper are two important tools to use when researching. When you find useful information, you should read it and take notes. This process is very important. It forces you to understand what you are reading and find the most relevant parts. When something makes sense, you can capture that understanding on paper. The process also helps you remember the information. Usually the written version of the information is shorter than the source, so the process reduces how much you will need to read when putting your project together.

Taking accurate notes can save time. So, check the spellings of the names of people and places, the dates of events, and the exact wording in direct quotes used in sources. You will not necessarily go back to the sources to double-check your notes later, so if you are not accurate, then you could make errors in your final report. Always make sure you write down the source, such as a web address or book title, preferably with a page or chapter number, so you know exactly where you found your information. This information will be crucial when you create the final project.

Yoruba
Lived in present-day southwestern Nigeria and Benin
No single capital city
Council of elders led by ruler called the oba
Lived in extended families in large villages
Farmers did not own land but occupied that of ancestors
Over 400 ancient gods and a prime mover and creator
*   called Olorun*

These are two sample fact cards with notes summarizing the differences between two West African tribes at the time of the slave trade.

Hausa
Lived in present-day northern Nigeria and southern Niger
No single capital city or hereditary ruler
Tribe leaders had strong links to Bayajidda, ancient founder of
*   the tribe*
Grew lots of indigo (used as dye) and cotton
Live in extended families in large villages
Farmers did not own land, but occupied that of ancestors
Islam main religion because Islamic traders came to region
*   from North Africa*

In your own words

The notes you take for a research assignment on slavery and the slave trade should be made in your own words, except for quotations, in order to avoid **plagiarism**. Plagiarism is using other people's words and their work as your own. It is a form of cheating. While some students accidentally use sections of material cut-and-pasted from the Internet in their essays, others cheat on purpose. Both forms of plagiarism are unacceptable.

Teachers can spot plagiarism by identifying if the words used do not seem like you wrote them, or if they recognize the source because they have looked at it themselves. They can type just a few sentences into an Internet search engine to confirm whether text has been copied from somewhere else. Schools punish or expel those who cheat.

How to avoid plagiarism

- Take notes as you read and record the source of the material.
- Mark any quotations as quotations so that you do not accidentally claim them as your own, and make sure to write the source next to them.
- If you like the way an author has said something, then use a phrase such as: "As Olaudah Equiano said, 'a scene of horror almost inconceivable' was found on slave ships."
- Never be tempted to plagiarize to save time!

The research journey

Research is a journey of discovery that can take time. Some possible sources of information will prove to be useless. Others are rich sources that lead to new sources that are just as useful. Links to other websites and page links in books can help you search further and get an overview more quickly than if you had to find all the sources yourself. If you find a source you like or trust, the links it contains may well take you to equally good information.

However, remember that your time is limited and that it is easy to get distracted from the research question. For example, say you are researching information on how the triangular trade started. You take notes from a relevant website, and you find links there to Frederick Douglass and abolition. Although these are interesting topics, they are not relevant to the development of the triangular trade. The transatlantic slave trade started in the 16th century, well before Douglass was even born.

The SQ3R technique

A useful aid to keep focused and stay on course during your research journey is the **SQ3R** technique. "SQ3R" stands for "**S**urvey, **Q**uestion, **R**ead, **R**ecite, **R**eview."

This technique helps you to find the relevance of evidence. It also helps you to remember by reading and reciting. Research is not a useful exercise if at the end you cannot remember why your evidence is important and how it fits into the overall framework of your assignment.

How to use the SQ3R technique

Survey ...
- a work's title, chapter, and spread headings and subheadings, as well as captions to pictures, charts, graphs, and maps.
- the foreword or introduction and conclusion or summary, looking for major ideas.
- review questions and educational study guides.

Question
- Turn the title, headings, and subheadings into questions.
- Ask yourself, "What question is this work (or section) trying to answer?"
- Read any questions that appear at the end of sections or chapters.
- Ask yourself, "What did my teacher say about this subject or chapter?"
- Ask yourself, "What do I already know about this subject?"

Read
- Look for answers to the questions that appear at the end of chapters or in an educational study guide.
- Reread captions to pictures, charts, graphs, and maps.

- Note all words or phrases that are underlined, italic, or bold.
- Read difficult passages more slowly.
- Stop and reread any passages that are not clear.
- Read a section at a time.

Recite
- Say questions out loud about what you have just read.
- Take notes from the text, but summarize the information in your own words.
- If using photocopies, underline or highlight important points you've just read.
- Recite answers out loud, remembering that the more focused your answers are, the more likely you are to remember what you read.

Review ...
- the key phrases and other notes you made within 24 hours of making the notes.
- again after one week.
- about once a month until the time of your presentation or exam.

Digging Deeper

The research skills you use to gain an overview of a topic would mostly apply to secondary sources. But once you complete this research, the next step is to fill in the missing pieces and to support ideas or themes in what you have found with specific examples. In order to dig deeper into history in this way, you will want to look in detail at primary sources. Primary sources are not only informative, but are also fascinating windows into the past.

Telephone

Have you played the game called Telephone? One person whispers something to someone else, who whispers what he or she thinks was said to someone else, and so on, until the message returns to the first person. Invariably the message has changed. We can think of secondary sources as being like the whispered messages, because the further you get from the original source of information, the greater is the chance of there being something wrong. Primary sources are like the original message. However, primary sources may be true or biased. That is why it is so important to have two sources for a piece of evidence to ensure it is reliable.

Slavery documents

There are many primary sources relating to slavery and the slave trade. Some are more **objective** than others because they do not include personal bias. Often the most important objective sources are official documents. For the topic of slavery, these might include:

- Ship records: Logbooks are like diaries of ship voyages. They give us some insight into the number of slaves transported across the Middle Passage as cargo and how many slaves got sick or died on the voyage. Manifests are lists of slaves completed at ports to show what ships carried.
- Slave merchant records: Official letters, account records, and ledgers (books detailing payments made by businesses and money received) tell us many things about the past. They give dates and details of slave markets and auctions. They show the flow of goods in the triangular trade. They also tell us about how slaves were valued. For example, they show how much slaves were sold for and how the physical condition of slaves affected the price.

- Plantation and estate records: Estate plans can show the layout of buildings, such as the huts in which slaves lived. Estate inventories were lists of what people owned. It is interesting to see how slaves featured on inventories, because they were considered to belong to plantation owners.
- Legal documents: Court records are official papers created during sessions of courts. They record punishments for slaves (for a detailed example, see page 28) and cases where people questioned whether it was legal to enslave other people. These sorts of cases were important in the abolition movement in the 18th and 19th centuries. Wills and testaments show the transfer of ownership of slaves when their owners died. Manumissions are rare legal documents that prove a slave had been freed.
- Slave registers: In the 19th century, U.S. slave owners had to register their slaves. The registers proved the slaves had been obtained legally and not as a result of the illegal slave trade. The registers are often detailed and record anything from a slave's name, skin color, and age through to his or her country of birth or job.

Slavery primary sources include 19th-century posters for slave sales. The sales were often held in the South in special auction houses like the one in the photograph.

Examining a primary source about slavery

The image on this page is an extract from court records from January 1814, written by a court official in Dominica in the Leeward Islands. In the early 19th century, these Caribbean islands were a British colony. The British government defended the islands from other countries' armed forces, controlled law and order, and gained wealth from the plantations in the region. Most of the population of Dominica was made up of African slaves who grew and processed the sugarcane on the plantations.

This extract shows an original court record from Dominica, described in the text.

This primary source provides lots of information for researchers into slavery. The first column gives the date when a slave appeared in court. The second gives the slave's name, and the third gives the slave's owner or the estate (plantation) that the owner ran. The fourth column lists the type of court session. In this extract, all slaves are facing a court martial, or military trial, which reveals that the court session was run by the British army. The fifth column lists the crime each slave was accused of and found guilty of doing. The sixth column reveals the punishment the court decided upon for each crime, and the seventh lists details about when the punishment was carried out.

Looking in detail

The names of the slaves include Rachel, Hector, Dick, and Jean-Pierre. They are British or French-sounding names, yet these people came from Africa. The document shows how slave owners gave first names to their slaves. The slaves do not have last names. It reminds us that slaves were considered possessions for slave owners, and their African past and heritage were disregarded.

The slaves' crimes seem to be rather petty to us today. For example, Hector was accused of being a runaway and Jean-Pierre was accused of attempting to return to the runaways with provisions. However, the sentences are incredibly harsh.

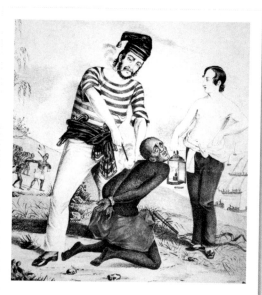

This drawing shows a slave being branded to show who owns him. Escaped slaves could be identified by these brands and then returned to their owners.

Hector received corporal punishment, or punishment by pain, for running away. He was whipped 100 times and forced to work in chains for six months. Jean-Pierre received capital punishment for his crime. He was not only hanged, but his head was cut off and put on a pole, and his body was hanged from a type of post called a gibbet.

This source is evidence of the importance to slave owners and the British government of the issue of runaways and rebellion. It opens up many questions for exploration. Why do you think runaways were seen as a threat to slavery on plantations? How could harsh punishment of runaways prevent further rebellion? How did rebellion spread through colonies in different places?

Runaways and rebellion

To find out more about the issue of runaway slaves, research the following:
- Cimarrones and Maroons
- Haitian Revolution
- Denmark Vesey and Nat Turner
- Events on the ship *Amistad* in 1839

Personal writing

Another category of primary sources gives a more personal interpretation of events, and is therefore more **subjective**. These primary sources include personal letters and diaries. For example, estate owners often corresponded with relatives about plantation life and kept diaries. These records detail life during the time of the slave trade, how slaves tried to escape, and what jobs they did. The sources also include autobiographies written by slaves, slave owners and traders, and other people who witnessed slavery firsthand. Here is an opening section from *Incidents in the Life of a Slave Girl*, the autobiography of Harriet Jacobs published in 1861:

"I was born a slave; but I never knew it till six years of happy childhood had passed away. My father was a carpenter, and . . . On condition of paying his mistress two hundred dollars a year, and supporting himself, he was allowed to work at his trade, and manage his own affairs. His strongest wish was to purchase his children; but, though he several times offered his hard earnings for that purpose, he never succeeded."

Autobiographies present facts and feelings told from one person's point of view. However, as in any published book, the final words used are not always those of the author. Books are edited for language and acceptability by other people. In the case of Jacobs's book, the editor and publisher rewrote some parts because they were considered too shocking for the readership. It is difficult to say anything is completely true based on accounts from centuries ago. Nevertheless, whether objective or subjective, primary sources such as these are invaluable to historians and researchers.

Who's who?

Authors sometimes write books under different names. There are various reasons for this. One is safety. For example, Harriet Jacobs was a runaway slave when she wrote her book and therefore risked punishment if she were caught. So she called herself Linda Brent in her book and changed the names of her master and other people to conceal her identity and avoid being caught by the authorities. Olaudah Equiano, who wrote one of the first slave autobiographies, was named Gustavus Vassa after being bought by a new master.

Where was Equiano from?

In the first part of his autobiography, *The Interesting Narrative of the Life of Olaudah Equiano, or Gustavus Vassa, the African*, published in 1789, Equiano describes his life in Africa. He claims he was born in 1745, one of seven children in an Ibo village in present-day Benin. His father was an elder or chief who helped solve village disputes. Equiano's descriptions of village life remain important to historians and researchers as some of the clearest and most detailed ever created by an African living at the time of the slave trade. Equiano claims he and his sister were kidnapped by another African tribe, the Aro. They were separated, and Equiano was sold as a slave several times to different Africans before being put aboard a slave ship destined for the North American colonies. In his book, Equiano describes the smells and other horrors of ship conditions in the Middle Passage:

"I was soon put down under the decks, and there I received such a salutation in my nostrils as I had never experienced in my life. . . . The closeness of the place, and the heat of the climate, added to the number in the ship, which was so crowded that each had scarcely room to turn himself, almost suffocated us."

Equiano's autobiography is an example of a primary source whose truth has been questioned.

Some people think these descriptions must be made up, based on several pieces of evidence from primary sources. For example, church records in London record Equiano's baptism as taking place in the British colony of Carolina in North America in 1759. If Equiano was born and not just baptized in Carolina, he would never have been on a slave ship. However, even if his descriptions are based on conversations with others, they are important to historians because there are very few other works in English from the mid-18th century about African culture and the slave trade.

Language difficulties

Old primary sources use the language, spellings, and handwriting conventions of the time. This can make them difficult to read for people today. For example, here is an extract from a slave ship's logbook with its original spelling: "This day died two men and 4 women haveinge many more sick, wee take the greatest care wee cann of them there is nothinge wantinge to them." Roughly this means: "Today two men and four women died, and many more slaves were sick. We take the greatest care of them we can, there is nothing we don't give them." Some words in primary sources are completely unfamiliar today. For example, the word "flux" meant "dysentery."

Sometimes when older primary sources are quoted in modern secondary sources, spellings and punctuation that are incorrect or unusual are often followed with [sic]. This tells us that they have been copied from the original, even though they wouldn't normally be used today. For example, it was common in slave sources from the 18th century to see black Africans and African Americans referred to as "Negroes," a word not used today because it is offensive.

Points of view

Many primary sources reveal strong points of view about slavery and the slave trade. These may seem shocking today because they were written in the past, when people had different attitudes about slavery and ideas about what was acceptable to say or do. People who wrote articles or books favoring slavery seem especially prejudiced.

Remember that in the Deep South of the United States, many people relied on slavery. They believed that slave labor was the main way individuals and states could get rich from plantation industries. Slavery also distinguished the South from the North. It was part of the southern identity of the time.

In the press

Newspapers and magazines from the 18th and 19th centuries are another type of primary source that can be useful when researching the slave trade. There were all kinds of periodicals around at that time. Daily papers included *The Times* of London, published from 1785 onward, and magazines such as *Harper's Weekly*. Regional titles included the pro-slavery *Savannah Gazette*, published in the South, and the abolitionist *North Star*, published in New

York. Newspaper articles are often shorter than magazine articles and summarize information in a small space. Articles are written by reporters whose job is both to tell the readers about what happened and to deliver interesting, popular stories that help sell copies. Thus, while slave rebellions were celebrated news for readers of *North Star*, they might be ignored or reported on in a way that warned plantation owners of trouble in newspapers from slave states. It is fascinating to compare the coverage of historical events in different periodicals.

THE SLAVE DECK OF THE BARK "WILDFIRE," BROUGHT INTO KEY WEST ON APRIL 30, 1860

Soon after the bark was anchored we repaired on board, and on passing over the side saw, on the deck of the vessel, about four hundred and fifty native Africans, in a state of entire nudity, in a sitting or squatting posture, the most of them having their knees elevated so as to form a resting place for their heads and arms. They sat very close together, mostly on either side of the vessel, forward and aft, leaving a narrow open space along the line of the center for the crew of the vessel to pass to and fro. About fifty of them were full-grown young men, and about four hundred were boys aged from ten to sixteen years. It is said by persons acquainted with the slave trade and who saw them, that they were generally in a very good condition of health and flesh, as compared with other similar cargoes, owing to the fact that they had not been so much crowded together on board as is common in slave voyages, and had been better fed than usual. It is said that the bark is capable of carrying, and was prepared to carry, one thousand, but not being able without inconvenient delay to procure so many, she sailed with six hundred.

Ninety and upward had died on the voyage. But this is considered as comparatively a small loss, showing that they had been better cared for than usual. Ten more have died since their arrival, and there are about forty more sick in the hospital. We saw on board about six or seven boys and men greatly emaciated, and diseased past recovery, and about a hundred that showed decided evidences of suffering from inanition, exhaustion, and disease. Dysentery was the principal disease. But notwithstanding their sufferings, we could not be otherwise than interested and amused at their strange looks, motions, and actions. The well ones looked happy and contented, and were ready at any moment to join in a song or a dance whenever they were directed to do so by "Jack"—a little fellow as black as ebony, about twelve years old, having a handsome and expressive face, an intelligent look, and a sparkling eye.

The underlined passages in this copy of an article from the magazine Harper's Weekly highlight the attitudes of the reporter toward slaves. He reports on this shocking scene with mild amusement and lack of concern for the slaves' suffering. The term "bark" (sometimes spelled "barque") refers to a type of sailing ship.

Every picture tells a story

Primary sources also include images, such as etchings and cartoons in periodicals, and prints, paintings, and drawings. Images include a wide range of subjects, from scenes of slave trading and plantation work to those of slave punishment and slave rebellion. Portraits show freed slaves and plantation families, and dramatized paintings show notable scenes, such as political moments in history or when slaves were thrown overboard from a slave ship. For example, Thomas Nast, a U.S. artist and supporter of Abraham Lincoln, produced famous images of Lincoln freeing slaves and of Lincoln's opponents encouraging slavery. Such images encouraged the U.S. public to elect Lincoln as president for a second term in 1864.

Slavery maps

Maps from different eras chart developments in the slave trade. In research you need to be aware that what maps show varies according to the year when they were created. Early European expeditions to Africa and the Americas created maps of the new territories they "discovered" and colonized. For example, maps of West Africa created in the 18th century show where different tribes lived and label coastal areas as "grain coast," "gold coast," and "ivory coast" because these were the goods traders could obtain from these areas. This map from a textbook shows which U.S. states outlawed and which permitted slavery in the run-up to the U.S. Civil War.

Many subjects in art from the past are not very realistic. For example, black Africans were often drawn with exaggerated features, such as big lips or startled eyes, and clearly not from observation of real people. This was much more marked in cartoons, which were popular in periodicals. Cartoons also mocked political figures of the day, such as Abraham Lincoln, and ideas, such as abolition. In one cartoon, a row of women look angry because they cannot have sugar in their tea, which some people argued would be a result of abolition.

Slave photographs

Photos of slaves and slave life are generally not available. There are several reasons for this. One is that photography only became available in the 1830s to 1840s and certainly was not widespread for many years. By that time the transatlantic slave trade and much of the slavery era was over.

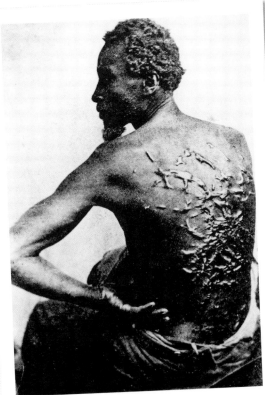

Another reason is that plantation owners in the South rarely wanted to document their slaves and work, since they were continuing a practice that was unpopular in Britain and much of the United States. Many photos of slaves were taken after they were freed or had escaped. Remember when you look at photos that, like other images, they are often subjective because

Photos, such as this one showing scars caused by repeated beatings, were taken by abolitionists as evidence of the cruelty of slavery.

they show what the photographer wants to include. For example, a photo of a slave family on a southern plantation may show several generations sitting happily together, but it would have been taken at a time when they were living in fear of separation and punishment. During research, always question why any image shows what it does.

Using images

Like text, images you discover in your research were created by someone. Therefore, if you find an image that helps your research, it is best to note what the image shows, where it is located, and why it is relevant. You might copy and paste the image from a website into a text document, save the web page as a favorite in your Internet browser, or photocopy an image from a book. It is important to write on any printouts of images where they came from, since you will need to acknowledge in your final work where you found any illustrations and that they were made by someone else.

Making a copy might be breaking the law of **copyright**, whereby only the person who created something can use it in publications. Publishers usually have to pay to use copyright images in their books. However, some images on the Internet can be used for educational purposes, and that includes your assignments. For example, images at http://hitchcock.itc.virginia.edu/Slavery/index.php are free to use for educational purposes.

Questioning primary sources

Part of the role of researchers is to question their sources. With primary sources, it is important to try to find out who made them and what they say. Individuals create primary sources when they draw a picture, send an email, or write a diary. Such documents and images are personal records. They might reflect whether someone is happy or sad, in favor of or against something, or concerned about or approving of someone. Sometimes it is obvious from historical primary sources what emotions the authors felt at that time, what was important to them, how they spoke, and what they thought was worth writing about or showing in an image.

However, not all primary sources are what they seem. They may look real, but are actually created in order to look old and be significant to historians. For example, slave tags were metal badges slave owners hung around their slaves' necks or wrists in the U.S. port of Charleston in the 19th century. Some people like to buy these **artifacts**, so other people make fake versions. Experts can spot these fakes because they are often stamped with the names of cities where slave tags were not issued.

The 5 Ws

Historians question whether sources are genuine and also their relevance to research goals by using the 5 Ws approach. This involves asking five questions about a source. These are: **W**hat is it? **W**ho created it? **W**hen did they create it? **W**here did they create it? And **W**hy did they create it? It is often difficult to answer all these questions about a source. But the process of questioning will help your understanding and interpretation.

It will force you to see the source in the context of the times in which it was made. Remember that your interpretation of what you find during research is important. Every individual and every generation creates a subtly different version of history.

What?

- What sort of source is it?
- What else might the author have in mind for this text?

Who?

- Who is the author of the text?
- Is the author an expert on the subject (for example, a historian)?
- Is a biography of the author included so you can learn more about her or him?

Where?

- Where did the information come from?

- Is the information biased?
- Does the information appear to be accurate?

When?

- When was the text written?
- Is the information as up-to-date as it needs to be (depending on your research question)?

Why?

- Why is this information useful to you?
- Why is this source useful, and is it better than others?

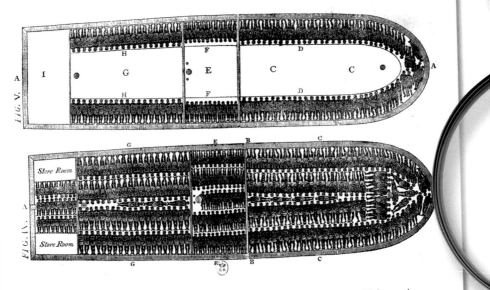

The plan of the overcrowded conditions on the slave ship Brooks is a widely used primary source image, just as it was widely used to promote abolition of slavery in the United Kingdom in the early 19th century. The arrangement of bodies was not based on real observations, but rather was made up using diagrams of the ship and accounts of how many slaves it usually carried.

Moving images

Filmmaking had not been invented during the time of slavery and the slave trade, yet movies and documentaries are a useful source for researchers into history. Movies have an advantage over photographs in that they can combine sound and images, and also may condense long periods of history into a short time frame. Filmmakers are experts in re-creating historical worlds. For example, the movie *Amistad* (1997) tells the real-life tale of a slave mutiny that took place on a slave ship in 1839. The movie then follows the court battles that followed, in which former president John Quincy Adams, among others, debated whether or not the escaped slaves—then in jail in the United States—should be granted their freedom and returned to Africa, or be treated as property and returned to slavery. (The slaves were eventually given their freedom.)

Historical inaccuracies and bias

When viewing any movie, even those that are documentaries or based on true stories, remember that filmmakers can be biased or make creative decisions about what to put in their work in order to tell a story that people will find easy to follow. For example, *Glory* (1989) is a movie about an African-American regiment fighting for the Union forces against the Confederate army (representing the slave states) in the U.S. Civil War. The movie is inaccurate because it portrays the soldiers as ex-slaves, yet army documents say that the soldiers were from free black families, some of whom were quite prominent in northern U.S. society in the 1860s.

Getting close to history

A final category of sources is real objects and places connected with slavery and the slave trade. Museums are the best places to see historical artifacts from the past, such as goods traded for slaves and equipment used to punish slaves. They may be displayed alongside maps of the slave trade, models of slave ships or plantations, pictures, and videos that set the objects in their context. The slave trade ports that grew rich from the triangular trade, such as Charleston, South Carolina, British cities such as Liverpool and Bristol, and Nantes in France, are good places to visit. There is often tourist information to help you discover sites associated with slavery. For example, In Charleston you can visit the Old Slave Mart where slaves were traded until the 1860s. In Liverpool you can follow a slavery trail passing buildings and streets associated with or named after slave traders. You may have the opportunity to visit places in the West Indies or West Africa with slave associations, such as Gorée Island in Senegal or James Island in Gambia, where slaves were held in dungeons prior to sailing for North Africa.

Many of us do not live near places with slave artifacts on display or cannot travel to places connected with the slave trade. However, anyone can view artifacts on the Internet. For example, you can view various slavery artifacts at http://research.history.org/JDRLibrary/Visual_Resources/VisualResourceFindingAids/Samplers/slavery.cfm, which includes details about the items displayed.

Primary source summary

- Primary sources range from official documents, which are the most objective, to autobiographies, pictures, and photographs, which are the most subjective.
- Analysis of primary sources is improved if you take into account the time in history when slavery and the slave trade existed, and read sources carefully. Look up any difficult or strange terms.
- Question any primary source by using the 5 Ws to discover whether they are useful in your assignment or not.
- Artifacts in museums or on the Internet can help bring slavery to life.

If you cannot visit museums connected with the slave trade, look online for pictures and information. This musket was a valuable item to trade with Africans who had no use for European money. It would have been exchanged for slaves.

Using Your Research

Once you have completed your research, it is time to use it for your assignment. It is important to keep focused on your research question or topic title. It is great to have lots of interesting and useful information, but how do you put it together to create a finished piece?

Organizing your notes

An important thing to remember about organizing research notes is that it will take time and concentration, just like the research itself. So, allow yourself time and space to get it done. Avoiding distractions is important so that you do not use the information in the wrong place or repeat it. A good way to start organizing is to divide your information into categories. You can organize it chronologically, according to when events significant to slavery occurred, or by ideas, such as different concepts of slavery. You can organize it by significant individuals, or by events in a particular country—for example, contrasting abolition history in the United States, United Kingdom, and Brazil. You can even organize it according to the type of evidence, or sources, that answer your question. The following sample spreadsheet summarizes notes on sources about the early Portuguese slave trade:

Source	What does this source show?	What does this source tell us about slavery?	What does this source tell us about the slave trade?
Description of a Portuguese sugar plantation on the coast of West Africa from the late 15th century	The Portuguese had set up sugar plantations in Africa growing sugar for Europe.	African slaves worked on Portuguese sugar plantations.	Slaves were used on sugar plantations off the coast of Africa.
16th-century engraving of Lisbon, Portugal, showing African slaves	Activities in big Portuguese cities, such as Lisbon, relied on slave labor.	Slavery happened in European cities.	There was a slave trade from Africa to Portugal, but it was not transatlantic at this time.

Making lists

Information on a large topic like slavery can be organized in many different ways. Some people create mental links between blocks of information by creating organized lists, or **outlines**, that contain written summaries of research. The research question or other assignment is given at the top of the outline and then is categorized by topic and subtopics within these. Topics themselves are numbered using Roman numerals, while subtopics are usually presented as indented points beneath the topic that are organized by letters or numbers. Information in outlines is limited to keywords.

Visualizing information

Graphic organizers are a pictorial way to organize research knowledge and ideas. They generally use simple shapes such as circles, squares, and lines to present information and show how it is related. In creating an organizer you will need to concentrate on the relationships between topics, which will help you to create new ideas and clarify your knowledge. One of the simplest graphic organizers is the timeline. This helps establish the order of events in a period of history. The general timeline on page 15 spans several centuries, but you can also create more detailed timelines for shorter periods to help you understand the course of events during that specific time.

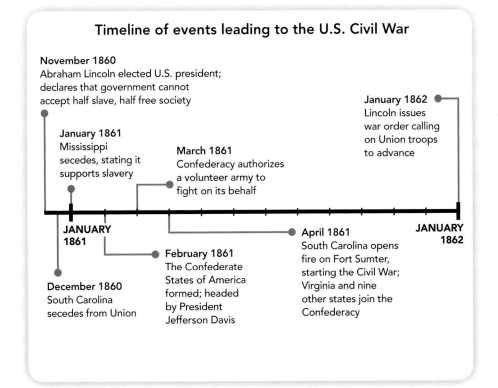

Timeline of events leading to the U.S. Civil War

November 1860
Abraham Lincoln elected U.S. president; declares that government cannot accept half slave, half free society

January 1861
Mississippi secedes, stating it supports slavery

March 1861
Confederacy authorizes a volunteer army to fight on its behalf

January 1862
Lincoln issues war order calling on Union troops to advance

JANUARY 1861

JANUARY 1862

December 1860
South Carolina secedes from Union

February 1861
The Confederate States of America formed; headed by President Jefferson Davis

April 1861
South Carolina opens fire on Fort Sumter, starting the Civil War; Virginia and nine other states join the Confederacy

Different organizers

There are many more styles of graphic organizer to choose from, depending on the kind of research information you have to organize.

Stars and spiders

Star diagrams are arranged like mind maps (see page 17), but have circles with supporting data, evidence, and other information radiating out from a single central research question or topic, such as "Slavery." Spider diagrams are a more detailed type of star, with lines of extra information from the radiating lines.

Fishbones

A fishbone diagram, or herringbone map, summarizes different aspects of a more complicated topic than could be used in a star diagram. An example of a more complicated topic that is interrelated with several subtopics is "Emancipation of slaves." This topic forms the head and backbone of the fishbone diagram. There are many complex reasons why some people in the 19th century wanted emancipation, from legal to economic. These subtopics or causes are linked to the central backbone of the diagram, from which parallel lines radiate as "ribs" with further details.

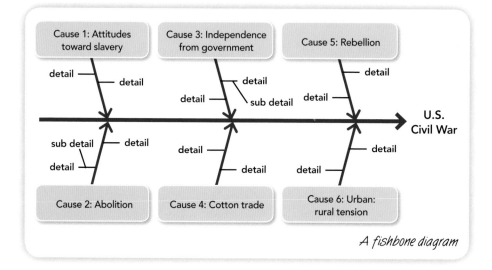

A fishbone diagram

Concept webs

Like fishbones, the central circle in a concept web might contain the research question, and arrows lead from this to smaller circles with subheads. Arrows lead from these to details or supporting facts, much like the way the word "slavery" leads to different ideas at the start of research (see the mind map on page 17).

Venn diagrams

A Venn diagram is made up of overlapping circles and is ideal for comparing and contrasting information of similar sorts, such as comparing different slave rebellions. For example, maybe you want to reveal contrasts between slave rebels Nat Turner and John Brown. The information individual to John Brown goes in one circle, information about Nat Turner goes in another circle, and information common to both goes in the overlapping part of each circle.

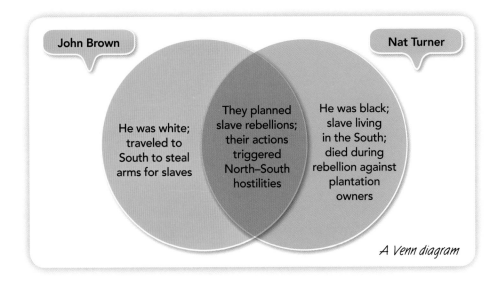

A Venn diagram

Flowcharts

Similar to timelines, flowcharts include information connected both chronologically and logically as steps in a chain. Here is an example of a flowchart for a slave rebellion:

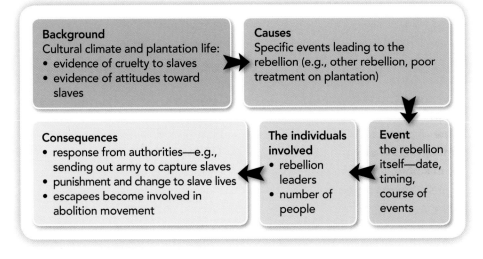

Consider the information

Organizing information helps you produce a plan for your work—a way to put together themes and blocks of information in your finished piece. As you put together graphic organizers and outlines, you may come across some information that does not quite fit the plan. For example, perhaps you have lots of information about the U.S. Civil War and how Union forces freed slaves as they defeated Confederate forces. You also have some information about the plight of freedmen (freed slaves) in the early 1860s. You found out that some freedmen moved from the South to the safety of Union states, but often ended up in crowded army stockades that had little food and where diseases spread. Some freedmen were hired out to Unionist farmers for very low wages.

This information does not back up the main point about the U.S. Civil War and slavery, namely that Union forces fought to end slavery and create better lives for the slaves they helped liberate. It is important to mention exceptions like this in your final report. Otherwise you are picking and choosing the historical evidence that you include and not telling the complete story.

Unexpected information

Here are some other pieces of information that might not necessarily fit some of the central ideas of slavery and the slave trade that you have discovered during research.

Africans helped European slave traders

Europeans exploited Africa only with the help of powerful Africans. They could not trade wherever they liked. They needed permission from the rulers of the kingdoms who controlled trading in their regions. Some were already trading in slaves, especially rulers on the eastern coast of Africa who traded slaves with people in the Middle East. Some African people formed alliances with Europeans because they brought armies and powerful weapons that could be employed to take territory from other African tribes.

People in northern states profited from slavery

Some ship owners in the North owned and continued to make money from operating slave ships right up to the second half of the 19th century. For example, the *Wildfire* mentioned in the piece on page 33 was a slave ship owned by a New Yorker. By the start of the 19th century, the percentage of free blacks increased in population censuses in New York City. However, there were also several thousand slaves in the city, serving in over 30 percent of New York City homes.

Some early black Americans had white servants

The first Africans arrived in the North American colonies in 1619. Most worked on tobacco plantations in Virginia as indentured servants. By the 1650s, some had bought their freedom and had their own farms. Some even paid for white servants to help produce their tobacco. By the early 18th century, laws had changed, and descendants of these early Americans were no longer allowed to raise crops for themselves or buy their freedom.

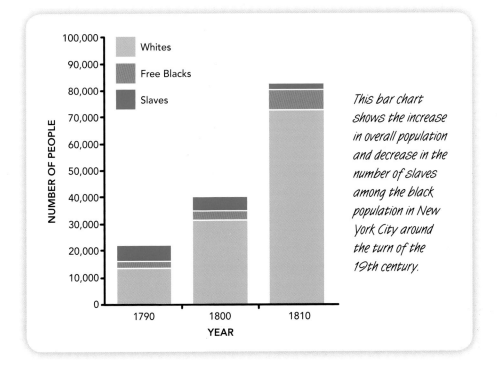

This bar chart shows the increase in overall population and decrease in the number of slaves among the black population in New York City around the turn of the 19th century.

The meaning of "Zong"

During slave trade research you may come across the "Zong" case. It refers to the infamous events on the slave ship HMS *Zong* in 1781. The captain ordered crew members to throw 133 sick, yet valuable, slaves overboard, for fear that other people on board would get sick. The boat owners then tried to claim money from insurers to pay for the missing slaves, saying there was not enough water to go around. A much publicized court case proved there was enough water. The case was used by abolitionists as proof that the slave trade should stop.

The role of individuals

An important background theme of any historical study is the role of individuals in changing the course of history. Secondary research sources often focus on particular people. During your research you will have found answers to questions such as: Why are they famous? What motivated them? What was the impact of the individual's life at the time, and is that impact viewed differently today?

One reason for discussing individuals in your finished piece is that their lives can sum up particular topics. For example, Harriet Tubman was an African-American woman famous for her role in organizing the Underground Railroad, which helped runaway slaves from the South get to the safety of the northern states in the 19th century. Tubman acted as a "conductor," organizing the secret network of black and white people who helped, sheltered, and fed the slaves on their journey to freedom. After abolition, Tubman campaigned for education and housing for freed slaves to help them live independent lives, and fought for civil rights for both African Americans and women. However, she, like other individuals, is only part of the story, so make sure you acknowledge the contributions of others, too, even if you do not discuss them in detail.

Getting ready to write

By now you will have planned out the structure of your assignment and will be getting ready to write. It is worth pausing before you start in order to consider a few things.

How long should your project be?

Often teachers or other people who assign your work will indicate how many words or pages they want you to write. In a multipart question, your teacher might specify what percentage of space you should dedicate to each part of the question. Pay close attention to the details of the assignment.

What format should you follow?

Obviously you will need to take different approaches depending on whether you are working on a project, writing an essay, or preparing an oral presentation.

Who is it for?

You will usually be expected to write for someone your age. This means using language you understand. If you had to write for a younger audience, you would need to use simpler words and shorter sentences.

Changing perception

The novel *Uncle Tom's Cabin* by Harriet Beecher Stowe was the second-best-selling U.S. book of the 19th century, after the Bible. It is about the lives of slaves and the cruelty of slave owners. The book is credited with encouraging the abolitionist movement in the 1850s. Abraham Lincoln said on meeting Stowe at the start of the U.S. Civil War: "So you're the little woman who wrote the book that made this big war." However, many people today think that, overall, the book had a negative impact on African Americans. The reason is that it created several common **stereotypes** for black people that persisted up to the 1960s. For example, Stowe's characters included dutiful, long-suffering, and rather childlike slaves who were devoted to their white masters or mistresses, such as Uncle Tom himself. This stereotypic perception of black people, which was widely accepted (especially in the South), may have slowed the progress of the U.S. civil rights movement during the early 20th century.

Harriet Tubman is pictured at far left. Her life story and actions sum up the enormous and complex process of change in U.S. society from the slave era to the start of the 20th century.

Frederick Douglass was a former runaway slave who established an anti-slavery newspaper and campaigned for civil rights in the United States. Douglass is a popular research subject for assignments about abolition.

Constructing your project

You will need to construct your project in ways that will help your reader follow what you are trying to say. Start with a single paragraph introduction that outlines what you will be writing about, stating the question or assignment title you have researched. Follow this with several paragraphs that provide the bulk of your work and contain the research information you have found from different primary and secondary sources. Each paragraph should have a different topic to demonstrate your understanding of events or arguments.

It is helpful to think of the acronym A-R-E to help you set out your arguments. "A" stands for assertion, which is the claim or statement, such as "John Brown was not a terrorist." The "R" is reasoning, or the reason why the assertion is true, such as "John Brown helped bring an end to slavery." "E" is evidence, or support for the assertion and reasoning, such as "the writings of abolitionists who used John Brown's efforts as inspiration." Evidence ranges from quotations and facts to illustrations.

Finally, include a conclusion paragraph to sum up your interpretation of evidence during the assignment. Remember that teachers and graders will have lots of similar assignments to read, so make yours stand out by making your points clear to the reader.

How to write

This book is not a guide to writing a finished piece. You know you are writing a nonfiction piece that will demand a different way of writing than a piece of fiction. So, there will be a limit to the use of descriptive words, opinions, and language suggesting feelings. You may feel strongly about slavery and slave-trade themes, but the job of a historical researcher is to be impartial, or unbiased. Therefore, hide your personal opinions or include opposing views to provide a balanced argument in your work. You could use sentence openers such as, "Many people today think that" and go on to say "but it is important to remember that during this period of history. . . " History does tell stories, so, like fiction, it has a strong narrative element. However, unlike fiction, it is supported by evidence. The likely place for persuasive language is the conclusion. This is where you may want to tell the reader, "This is why it appears that . . . "

Quotations

Quotations provide evidence and show that your ideas are based on research. Present quotations by copying them accurately inside quotation marks. Follow the quotation with the author's name and the year when the source was published. Some historical quotes are long, so include only what you need to support your point—usually one or two sentences. You can replace words you want to cut out with an ellipsis, or three dots in a row (. . .), to show the reader there is something missing. For example, compare the following versions of a quote by William Lloyd Garrison, the U.S. abolitionist. The second version has the same "demand," but without the detail about the slaves in the country.

"I demand the immediate emancipation of all who are pining in slavery on the American soil, whether they are fattening for the shambles in Maryland and Virginia, or are wasting, as with a pestilent disease, on the cotton and sugar plantations of Alabama and Louisiana; whether they are males or females, young or old, vigorous or infirm. I make this demand, not for the children merely, but the parents also; not for one, but for all; not with restrictions and limitations, but unconditionally."

"I demand the immediate emancipation of all who are pining in slavery on the American soil . . . not for one, but for all; not with restrictions and limitations, but unconditionally."

Give credit

The information in any source was put together by an individual or group of people. The material they produced will help you complete your assignment or other task. So, it is only right that you acknowledge in your bibliography the sources you mention or cite in the text, such as where you got quotes from, and also sources you read and used but did not cite. In a picture list, many people cite the source and page number or website where the illustration appears.

How to cite a source

It is usual to list items in your bibliography in alphabetical order by author name. This system is commonly used in libraries and educational centers because it is logical and readers can easily find names. You should supply as much of the following information as possible:

- author's last name, followed by first name or initials
- title of book, article, or web page
- edition and/or volume number that could help others locate the source
- place of publication and name of publisher
- year of publication or date of access for websites, whose content can change over time, unlike books.

Bibliography entries

Here are some examples of the different ways to cite books, magazines, encyclopedias, and websites:

Book
Hatt, Christine. *Questioning History: The African-American Slave Trade.* Mankato, Minn.: Smart Apple Media, 2004.

Magazine article
Trout, R. A. "Freedom Railroad." *Slavery Review,* no. 22 (2007): 3–15.

Encyclopedia
Encyclopedia Britannica. 15th ed. s.v., "Slavery."

Website
Shakir, Nancy. "Slavery in New Jersey." Slavery in America. www.slaveryinamerica.org/history/hs_es_jersey.htm (accessed June 1, 2009).

Footnotes and endnotes

Some people choose to refer to their sources in the body of their report near where they were used. They mark them with a small raised number (like this[1]), an asterisk (*), or a dagger (†). The number or mark draws attention to a footnote at the bottom of the page or end of a section. The footnote may cite the source as in a bibliography, or include a shorter version of a source listed in full in the bibliography. Endnotes are like footnotes, but the reference marks refer to numbered items in a list at the end of the work. Most word-processing programs, such as Word, can help you create and organize footnotes and endnotes. Make sure you follow the citation method your teacher wants you to use.

Check and edit

You have reached the final stage in preparing your assignment. You have organized your text into paragraphs and laid them out neatly using word-processing or page-making software. You have added images that help illustrate your topic. All that is left to do is the final check. This is essential in avoiding errors. Some of the obvious things to check are the number of words, which you can check automatically in any word-processing program, the spellings, and the sense of sentences and paragraphs. Ideally get someone else to read it, too. Often you have spent so much time on the work and are so familiar with the research you used in preparing it that you cannot spot any problems. Finally, carefully edit the assignment. For example, if you have to cut the number of words, make sure you do not change the meaning of sentences.

Summary

- Organize your notes with the help of graphic organizers and outlines.
- Structure your assignment carefully using paragraphs.
- Use quotes carefully and cite sources.
- Cite all research sources in a bibliography and picture list.
- Check, edit, and refine your assignment before handing it in.

Glossary

abolish/abolition ending of something through banning it by law. Abolitionists were people who worked to abolish slavery.

artifact human-made object that gives clues about how people lived in the past

baptism ritual using water that people take part in to become members of a Christian church

bias prejudice, or with an inclination toward a particular point of view

chattel slavery form of slavery in which a slave is treated as a piece of property, belonging to his or her owner, and has no rights

citation reference to where information comes from

civil war war between groups of people within the same country. The U.S. Civil War was fought between the North and the South during 1861–65.

colonial relating to an area or country in one country that is ruled by people in another country. Slavery was common on colonial plantations.

copyright legal right of ownership of a work or image

database online tool a researcher can use, containing information from a range of sources and links that are selected for a specific audience. Most are subscription services that require membership or payment.

emancipated freed from slavery

free state refers to any U.S. state that prohibited slavery prior to the U.S. Civil War

graphic organizer diagram that shows the relationships between ideas

human rights every person's legal or moral rights

indentured servant person voluntarily or involuntarily contracted to work for someone for a fixed number of years

indigenous from the local area

Industrial Revolution rapid development of industry using machines in the late 18th and early 19th centuries, which started in the United Kingdom

KWL chart table that shows what someone **K**nows about a topic, what he or she **W**ants to know about it, and what he or she has **L**earned about it

Middle Ages time in European history from about 500 CE to 1500

Middle Passage middle section of the journey slaves were forced to make from Africa to North America, which included a dangerous trip across the Atlantic Ocean

mind map diagram that begins with the main idea or keyword in the center and then has linked words or ideas radiating out

New World the Americas. The Old World includes Europe and Africa.

objective when something is viewed neutrally, without personal bias

outline method of organizing information using numbers and letters to indicate the main topics, as well as the subtopics under each main point

plagiarism claiming someone else's words or thoughts as your own

plantation large farm or estate, especially in a tropical or semitropical country, on which crops such as cotton, tobacco, and coffee are grown

primary source actual historical record, contemporary to the period when it was produced

scanning technique used to find specific information by quickly reading down a page looking for keywords, words in bold type, or headings

secede withdraw from something. Southern states seceded from the United States at the beginning of the U.S. Civil War.

secondary source research material or source that contains information based on another primary or secondary source

segregated separated from others because of race or religion

skimming reading technique used to determine if the material being read contains information that can answer a question

slave state refers to any U.S. state where slavery was legal and widespread prior to the U.S. Civil War

SQ3R stands for "Survey, Question, Read, Recite, Review." This technique guides you through finding evidence and also remembering it through reading and reciting.

stereotype oversimplified image or opinions about a person or group of people

subjective judgment based on personal impressions, feelings, and opinions rather than facts

triangular trade slave trade routes that linked Africa, the New World colonies, and Europe. Slaves were carried from Africa to North America, and sugar, tobacco, and other products were transported to Europe.

Underground Railroad secret routes and safe houses used by 19th-century slaves in the United States to escape in the years before the U.S. Civil War

Find Out More

Books

Cameron, Ann, and Olaudah Equiano. *The Kidnapped Prince: The Life of Olaudah Equiano.* New York: Random House, 2005.

Hatt, Christine. *Questioning History: The African-American Slave Trade.* Mankato, Minn.: Smart Apple Media, 2004.

Haugen, Brenda. *Frederick Douglass: Slave, Writer, Abolitionist.* Minneapolis: Compass Point, 2005.

Riehecky, Janet. *Point of Impact: The Emancipation Proclamation, the Abolition of Slavery.* Chicago: Heinemann Library, 2002.

Taylor, Marian, and Heather Lehr Wagner. *Harriet Tubman: Antislavery Activist.* Philadelphia: Chelsea House, 2005.

Taylor, Yuval, ed. *Growing Up in Slavery: Stories of Young Slaves as Told By Themselves.* Chicago: Lawrence Hill, 2005.

Vickers, Rebecca. *History in Literature: The Story Behind Mark Twain's Adventures of Huckleberry Finn.* Chicago: Heinemann Library, 2007.

Websites

General websites about slavery

www.slaveryinamerica.org

This detailed website provides information about the history of slavery in the United States, the geography of slavery, and more.

www.slavevoyages.org

This website about the transatlantic slave trade has an extensive database of information, including information on specific voyages and the names of specific slaves.

www.afroam.org/history/slavery/index.html

This is the home page of an interactive website about slavery from the Black History Museum.

www.pbs.org/wgbh/aia/home.html

This well-illustrated resource documents slavery in the United States in four parts.

www.pbs.org/wnet/slavery/

This website includes information about the lives of slaves, with many firsthand accounts.

http://hitchcock.itc.virginia.edu/Slavery/index.php

This website contains a visual record of the transatlantic slave trade and slave life in the Americas and provides many images related to slavery.

Rebellion and abolition

www.nationalgeographic.com/features/99/railroad/
   National Geographic's well-illustrated site explores the Underground
   Railroad.

www.iupui.edu/~douglass/
   This site includes a general history of the abolitionist movement in the
   United States, centered on Frederick Douglass, with firsthand accounts of
   former slaves, travel notes, diaries, illustrations, and memoirs.

http://rmc.library.cornell.edu/abolitionism/abolitionists.htm
   This detailed website explores abolitionism in the United States.

www.slaveryinamerica.org/geography/slave_insurrections.htm
   Use this website to explore the geography of slavery and slave rebellions
   and insurrections in the United States.

www.osv.org/explore_learn/document_viewer.php?DocID=2021
   This account tells of a free African-American childhood in New England in
   the 19th century.

Primary sources

http://memory.loc.gov/ammem/snhtml/snhome.html
   Read some of the 2,300 first-person accounts of slavery from the
   Federal Writers' Project.

http://antislavery.eserver.org
   This source of primary material includes essays and speeches by people
   on the anti- and pro-slavery sides in the United States.

www.archives.gov/index.html
   The National Archives and Records Administration site contains some
   important primary sources, such as Lincoln's Emancipation Proclamation of
   1863 and the Thirteenth Amendment of 1865 (the abolition of slavery).

www.pbs.org/wgbh/aia/rb_index_hd.html
   This web page links to all kinds of historical documents related to the
   topic of slavery.

http://lcweb2.loc.gov/ammem/aap/aaphome.html
   "African-American Perspectives" is a section of the Library of Congress
   website with a wealth of primary sources, from abolitionist speeches to
   accounts of lynchings of African Americans at the end of the 19th century.

Index